D0845971

Grand Teton National Park

PRESERVING AMERICA

Nate Frisch

Published by
CREATIVE EDUCATION AND CREATIVE PAPERBACKS

P.O. Box 227, Mankato, Minnesota 56002
Creative Education and Creative Paperbacks are imprints of The Creative Company
www.thecreativecompany.us

Design and production by Danny Nanos of Gilbert & Nanos
Art direction by Rita Marshall
Printed in Malaysia

Photographs by Alamy (DIZ Muenchen GmbH, Sueddeutsche Zeitung Photo), Corbis (Atlantide Phototravel, Corbis), Dreamstime (Steve Estvanik, Sergey Lavrentev), National Park Service, Shutterstock (Lester Balajadia, bikeriderlondon, Steve Byland, catwalker, CLS Design, Sharon Day, Dennis W. Donohue, Dean Fikar, Stacy Funderburke, gary718, IDAK, Images by Dr. Alan Lipkin, Jody Ann, James Mattil, MBoe, Nagel Photography, Lee O'Dell, pashabo, pisaphotography, Lee Prince, Ratikova, Tom Reichner, Terry Reimink, RONORMANJR, Phillip Rubino, sezer66, silky, Debbie Steinhausser, Tim Stirling, Sue Stokes, This World Photography, Dan Thornberg, Beth Trudeau, visceralimage, Peter von Bucher, Krzysztof Wiktor)

Library of Congress Cataloging-in-Publication Data

Frisch, Nate.
Grand Teton National Park / Nate Frisch.
p. cm. — (Preserving America)
Includes bibliographical references and index.
Summary: An exploration of Grand Teton National Park, including how its mountainous landscape was formed,
its history of preservation, and tourist attractions such as the waterfall known as Hidden Falls.

ISBN 978-1-60818-606-8 (hardcover)
ISBN 978-1-62832-181-4 (pbk)
1. Grand Teton National Park (Wyo.)—Juvenile literature. I. Title.
F767.T3F75 2015
978.7'55—dc23   2014028059

CCSS: RI.5.1, 2, 3, 8; RI.6.1, 2, 3, 4, 5, 6, 7; RH.6-8.4, 5, 6, 7, 8

First Edition HC 9 8 7 6 5 4 3 2 1
First Edition PBK 9 8 7 6 5 4 3 2 1

Cover & page 3: *Mt. Moran and Oxbow Bend; an osprey*

CREATIVE EDUCATION • CREATIVE PAPERBACKS

Grand Teton National Park

Nate Frisch

Table of Contents

TOWERING MOUNTAINS and glassy lakes. Churning rivers and dense forests. Lush prairies and baking deserts. The open spaces and natural wonders of the United States once seemed as limitless as they were diverse. But as human expansion and development increased in the 1800s, forests and prairies were replaced by settlements and agricultural lands. Waterways were diverted, wildlife was overhunted, and the earth was scarred by mining. Fortunately, many Americans fought to preserve some of the country's vanishing wilderness. In 1872, Yellowstone National Park was established, becoming the first true national park in the world and paving the way for future preservation efforts. In 1901, Theodore Roosevelt became U.S. president. He once stated, "There can be no greater issue than that of conservation in this country," and during his presidency, Roosevelt signed five national parks into existence. The National Park Service (NPS) was created in 1916 to manage the growing number of U.S. parks. In 1929, Grand Teton National Park was established in western Wyoming. Featuring some of the most spectacular mountainscapes in the world, this valley preserve has become renowned for its breathtaking scenery, larger-than-life animals, and diverse forms of recreation.

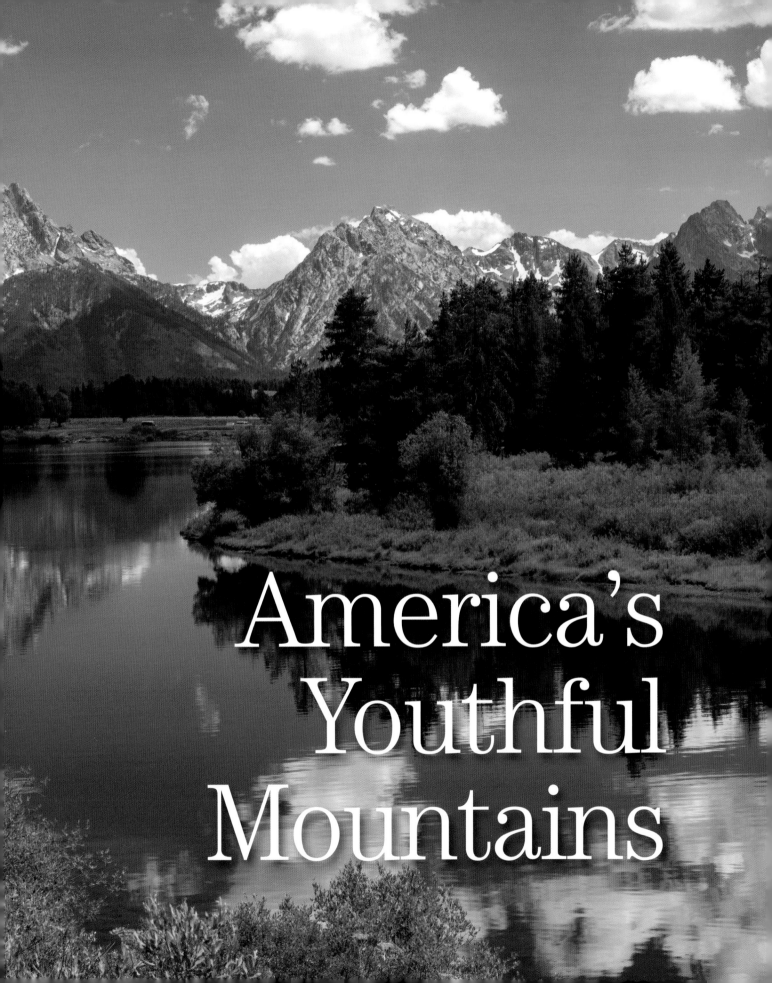

America's Youthful Mountains

"America the Beautiful"—one of the most beloved patriotic songs of the U.S.—extols the natural wonders of the nation. The first verse speaks of "purple mountain majesties above the fruited plain." These words could easily be describing the Teton Range of western Wyoming. Here, sharply defined peaks rise above a valley floor to the east. Grassy prairies abruptly transition to exposed mountainsides that shift from hues of purple and blue to tan and white, depending on the season, weather, and time of day. By comparison, most mountains are more irregularly shaped, feature **foothills** with gradual vegetation transitions, and are dirtier looking. The Teton Range is different for a few reasons, including its age, formation process, and glacial sculpting. The Rocky Mountains, or Rockies, in which the Teton Range is located, stretch 3,000 miles (4,828 km) from New Mexico to northern Canada and began forming about 80 million years ago. **Tectonic** plates in the earth's crust shifted, with some sliding underneath others in a process called subduction. This resulted in a huge ridge of fractured, elevated land. Further tectonic activity reshaped the Rockies in the millennia that followed, and many sub-ranges developed.

Around 10 million years ago, pressure and movement inside the earth pushed and pulled layers of rock in opposite directions. This caused a fault, or break, to occur near the present-day border of Wyoming and Idaho. The western side of the fault tilted up, while the eastern side collapsed. When the dust settled, the raised section peaked at more than 13,770 feet (4,197 m) above sea level, forming the Teton Range. The lower section became a valley, sitting 7,000 feet (2,134 m) below the new mountaintops. Among the most prominent summits of the 40-mile (64.4 km) range were 5 consecutive peaks referred to as the Cathedral Group. Their impressive height is visually amplified by lower canyons that bookend the group on the north and south ends. The tallest peak in the group is named Grand Teton.

When the Teton Range lifted, the existing surface layers of crust tilted west. So the western slopes are more gradual, and they are covered with softer rock that had been exposed to **erosion** and plant growth prior to the break. The eastern slopes are steep and composed of hard **metamorphic** gneiss and **igneous** granite that had been deep

Below the Tetons, lush floodplains formed along the Snake River in park areas such as Schwabacher's Landing (pictured).

underground for 2.7 billion years. Granite is resistant to wind and water erosion, and what little stone wears away cascades to the bottom of the slope. This is why the Tetons have such smooth-looking peaks and why foothills have never built up.

The only erosive forces that had a significant impact in the eastern slopes were glaciers. About 2 million years ago, these massive ice sheets began as solidly packed snow that built up under their own weight. Gravity worked to pull the glaciers down the mountainsides, and rock broke up in their paths. The loosened rock was then dragged along like sandpaper, further sculpting the granite. This ultimately left U-shaped canyons in the mountainsides. It also cleared the Tetons of vegetation. The glaciers would slow or stop when they reached the bases of the mountains, but their weight still served to flatten the valley floor or create depressions that would later fill with water and become lakes.

As the world's climate warmed up, most glaciers in the Tetons thawed, but some still exist among the mountaintops. Today, rain and snowmelt follow the glacial grooves and canyons of the eastern slopes, often plummeting as waterfalls to the valley below. That valley is now known as Jackson Hole. On the opposite side of Jackson Hole are the Gros Ventre and Washakie ranges. While they are shorter, gentler, and less visually striking than the Tetons, they serve an important purpose: they channel additional moisture into the valley. Most of this water flows into the Snake River or one of many glacial lakes. Jackson Hole's largest body of water, Jackson Lake, covers about 40 square miles (104 sq km) at the northern end of the valley. The Snake River enters and exits Jackson Lake before weaving south. The presence of lakes, streams, and ponds helps support a variety of **ecosystems**.

Living in the bodies of water are numerous fish species, including

Fish-eating ospreys (above) take advantage of the prey contained in the many mountain lakes of the Tetons.

From the powerful elk (above) to the clever beaver (opposite), 61 mammal species enjoy Grand Teton's lands and waters.

five species of trout. The fish provide food for bald eagles, osprey, and river otters. Lake, pond, and river shorelines also support leafy plants and bushes as well as willow and cottonwood trees. These areas are favored by moose, beavers, trumpeter swans, frogs, and a few snake species.

Expanses of sagebrush mixed with grasses and wildflowers cover most of the valley floor. Pronghorn graze in these areas, and coyotes and badgers hunt for burrowing rodents. Forests dominated by lodgepole pines often stand between the sagebrush and the bare mountainsides. These forests conceal elk, mule deer, gray wolves, black bears, and grizzly bears. Most of these animals actually move among forests, wetlands, and grasslands to feed but prefer the cover of the forest when resting. The scarcely vegetated mountains are inhabited by only a handful of hardy species, including bighorn sheep and American pikas.

All life in the Tetons and Jackson Hole must either be adapted to cold, snowy weather or able to move away from it. The average low temperature during the winter months is 2 °F (-16.7 °C) in Jackson Hole, and 14 feet (4.3 m) of snow falls annually. Temperatures are colder yet in higher elevations. Summer months often hit highs of 80 °F (26.7 °C), but nighttime temperatures still drop near freezing.

The first humans to see the Tetons did so about 11,000 years ago when the last **glacial period** was coming to an end. They were called Paleo-Indians and most likely hunted, caught fish, and gathered edible plants and berries in the lower elevations during the summers. Ever since then, the valley has remained important to native people, and in more recent centuries, the area was used or inhabited by Shoshone, Blackfoot, Crow, Nez Perce, Gros Ventre, Bannock, and Flathead tribes. The mountain valley was valued not only for its resources but also for its beauty, and the Tetons were considered sacred by many Indians. Some tribes that lived elsewhere would visit purely for spiritual reasons.

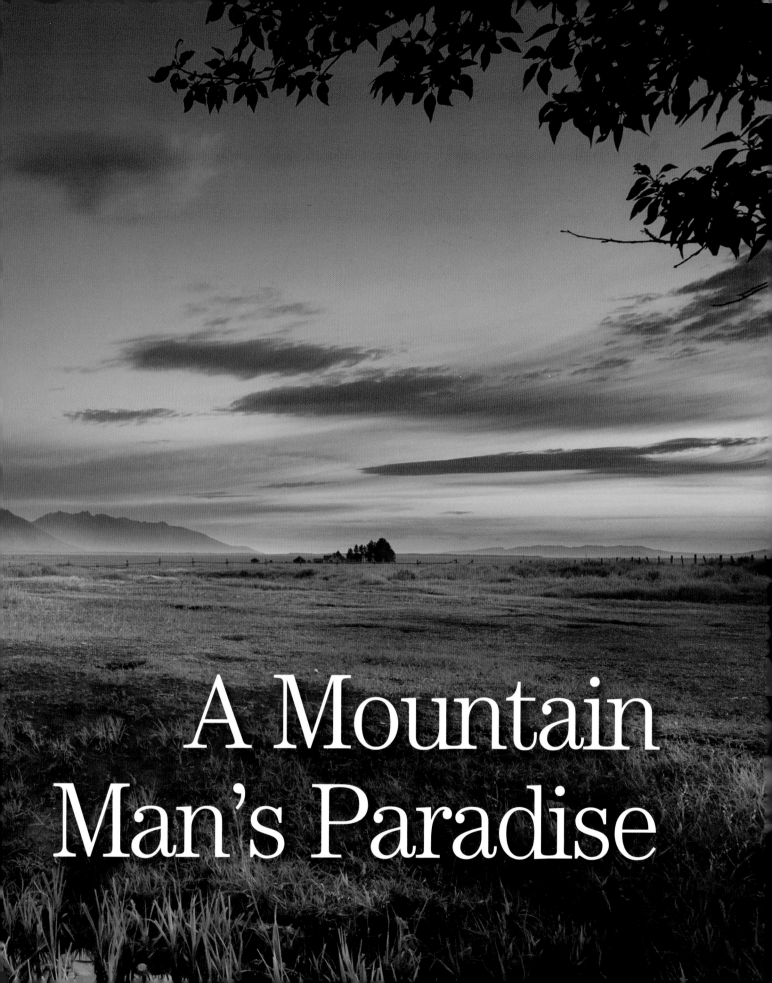

A Mountain Man's Paradise

In the late 1700s, events were unfolding far to the east that would ultimately change life among the Tetons. With the official end of the American Revolutionary War in 1783, the U.S. became an independent nation. But at that point, it did not extend west of the Mississippi River. Then, in 1803, the U.S. made a $15-million deal with France. The Louisiana Purchase roughly doubled the size of the country overnight, and the U.S. government—namely president Thomas Jefferson—was eager to learn more about this wild land that was still mysterious to European immigrants.

The Corps of Discovery, led by Meriwether Lewis and William Clark, began an expedition in 1804 that would follow the Missouri River northwest and then continue across the West all the way to the Pacific Coast. The expedition passed well north of the Tetons on its way to the ocean, but on the return trip, John Colter—a scout, hunter, and trapper—asked to leave the company to join a pair of trappers it had encountered. Colter navigated mountains well, and his pursuit of furs led him to Teton's eastern valley in 1807 or 1808.

Colter did not heavily publicize the valley, but beaver pelts were highly prized for women's fashions in the early 1800s, and his success attracted more trappers to the area during the following decades. One such trapper who favored the region was David Edward "Davey" Jackson, and in the late 1820s, the sunken valley was dubbed "Davey Jackson's Hole"—a name that would later be shortened to "Jackson's Hole" and then simply "Jackson Hole." By 1840, beaver populations were dwindling, and the pelts were no longer fashionable back east. The trappers left, and for the next couple of decades, the Indians had the Tetons and Jackson Hole to themselves again.

In 1860, an expedition slated to explore the Yellowstone region

Lewis and Clark's expedition, covering more than 8,000 miles (12,875 km), helped spark settlement in the American West.

was forced south to Jackson Hole by the snowy weather, and so the Tetons and the valley were officially explored for the first time. When the American Civil War broke out the following year, though, all thoughts of western investigations were put on hold.

Beginning in 1871, geologist Ferdinand Hayden led two Yellowstone expeditions that also explored parts of Jackson Hole. Hayden's parties included photographers and painters as well as **topographers**, **botanists**, and biologists. His expeditions yielded both scientific and artistic evidence of the area's magnificence and were largely responsible for the establishment of Yellowstone National Park in 1872. But Jackson Hole and the Tetons received no such designation.

Incidentally, it was during one of Hayden's expeditions that Jackson Hole's Leigh Lake and Jenny Lake were given their titles. A British immigrant named Richard Leigh and his Shoshone wife Jenny resided near the Tetons and had assisted Hayden's group. The couple's insider knowledge of the land proved so valuable that the party named the lakes in their honor.

Jackson Hole's surrounding peaks keep heavy, snow-chilled air from escaping the valley, resulting in frigid winter temperatures.

Today 65 feet (20 m) high, the concrete Jackson Lake Dam was rebuilt in the 1980s to protect it against future earthquake damage.

An 1876 exploration down the Snake River should have shed more light on Jackson Hole and the Tetons, but it was first delayed by bitter weather and then foiled by white-water rapids that destroyed the party's boat. The terrible voyage almost killed the crew and did little to enhance knowledge or appreciation of the region.

The first homesteaders in Jackson Hole staked their claims in 1884. The broad valley with its lakes and streams appeared promising for agricultural use, but sandy soil, long winters, and dry summers proved otherwise. Predators such as wolves and bears were also potential threats to livestock. These predators were trapped or shot by residents, and, in the early 1900s, Jackson Lake was dammed up to supply more water to nearby Idaho.

Although the region was changing, the area's aesthetic draw was unmistakable, and when wealthy Easterners began coming as sightseers in the early 1900s, struggling ranchers shifted their business toward tourism. Soon, **dude ranches** were giving urban dwellers a natural, old-fashioned experience. Around the same time, Yellowstone officials and other conservationists were pushing to expand Yellowstone's borders to include part of the Teton Range as well as the north end of Jackson Hole.

When the NPS was formed in 1916, director Stephen Mather and his assistant Horace Albright wasted little time in working up a plan for Yellowstone's expansion. Wyoming legislators contributed to the bill, and after receiving approval from the U.S. House of Representatives, the park expansion seemed imminent. But at the next level, the U.S. Senate, Idaho senators argued against the expansion, saying it would cut into important grazing areas that Idaho ranchers were presently permitted to use. The bill was shot down.

In truth, it was not only ranchers who opposed the park expansion but also local businesses, dude ranch owners, and anyone else who feared a federally operated park might diminish their tourism profits. The area remained open to private purchase and use, and, by the 1920s,

Early 20th-century residents visited Menor's Ferry General Store, now open to customers inside the park's historic district.

hotels, gas stations, dance halls, and even racetracks littered the valley. At the same time, once-prolific animals such as wolves were on the verge of being wiped out by hunting and land development. And talk of damming more lakes had begun.

Suddenly, local businesses that had opposed government protection of the land grew concerned about overdevelopment. They wanted to keep Jackson Hole as it was at that moment. Specifically, they wanted existing grazing, hunting, and business operations to continue but wanted restrictions on new development and business competition. Designated national forest land around Jackson Hole had the types of regulations that locals wanted, as the rules limited private land purchase but allowed existing activities to continue. However, the federal government would not impose the same regulations throughout Jackson Hole, since much of the valley was not forested. The locals' next option was to buy up as much private land as they could to prevent newcomers from moving in.

This plan took a hit in 1926, when a man with purer motives toured the area. John D. Rockefeller Jr. came from an extremely wealthy family that had made a fortune in the oil industry. The Rockefellers were known for their generosity to causes they thought were worthwhile. Rockefeller was in awe of the Teton Range as well as the forests, prairies, and lakes at its foot. Guiding the **philanthropist** through the area was Albright, now the Yellowstone National Park superintendent. Albright was well

Present-day Jackson Hole (above) continues to welcome visitors to the park, decades after Rockefeller's (right) intervention.

aware of the local objections and political obstacles involved in expanding or establishing a national park in the area, and he informed Rockefeller of the challenges. Rockefeller did what he could and ultimately purchased 55 square miles (142 sq km) of private land in Jackson Hole with the intent of donating the property for future national park use. However, he made his purchase under a made-up company name—the Snake River Land Company—so that locals wouldn't know that he was behind all the dealings.

Within a few years, a national park seemed inevitable. But resistant locals still held sway. Instead of a Yellowstone expansion, a smaller, localized park was preferred, presumably because a small, upstart park would present less competition than the large, well-established Yellowstone. In addition, scattered plots of land still owned by private residents and businesses in Jackson Hole would restrict park boundaries.

In 1929, the establishment of Grand Teton National Park was approved by both the House and the Senate and then by president Calvin Coolidge. The 150-square-mile (388 sq km), irregularly shaped park included little of the Jackson Hole valley, but it did contain a 25-mile (40.2 km) stretch of the Teton Range, including the Cathedral Group, and 6 lakes at the base of the range—Jenny and Leigh lakes among them.

Political Strife and New Wildlife

The new national park was far from ideal. It mostly "protected" mountains, and while some lakes were managed, Jackson Lake, the Snake River, and many smaller waterways and lakes were not included within the park's confines. The park also included very limited portions of forests or sagebrush. Immediate efforts were made to expand the park so that it would preserve not only inorganic nonliving scenery but also living ecosystems.

Opposition arose again. Apart from the usual complaints, Teton County argued about losing tax money, the U.S. Forest Service (USFS) didn't want to give up forest control to the NPS, and the state of Wyoming objected to its land resources being claimed at the whim of the federal government. Multiple bills to expand the park were introduced in the mid-1930s, but they all failed. Opposing sides continued the battle into the late '30s and early '40s.

In December 1941, the U.S. joined World War II. This cast more doubt on a Grand Teton expansion, because the federal government's priorities turned toward the war effort and industrial progress and away from conservation. Then, in 1943, Rockefeller stepped in again. The land he had bought for park use nearly 20 years earlier still was not included in Grand Teton's boundaries. A frustrated Rockefeller decided to go over the heads of the bickering parties and wrote a letter directly to president Franklin D. Roosevelt. Rockefeller informed the president that if the U.S. government would not accept and use Rockefeller's freely offered property, he would simply sell it off to other buyers.

This ultimatum paid off, and Roosevelt used the authority granted him by the Antiquities Act to create Jackson Hole National Monument. The area included Rockefeller's donated land plus a great deal more, totaling 345 square miles (894 sq km). Its western border came up

After Franklin D. Roosevelt's (above) approval of a national monument, Grand Teton National Park took shape (opposite).

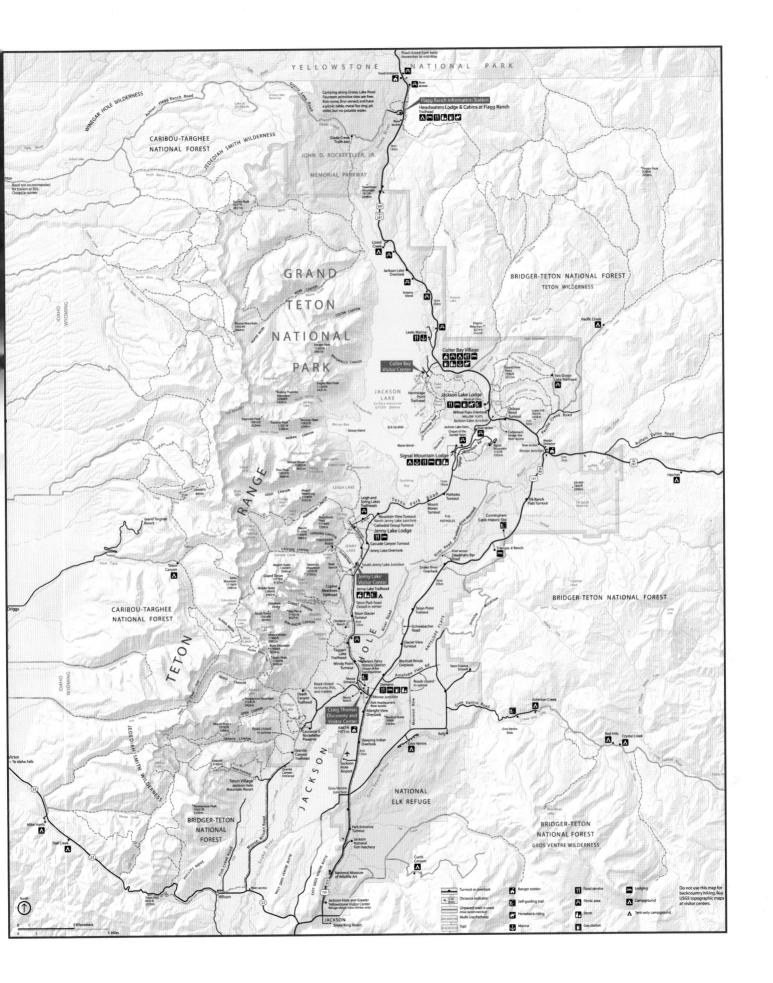

against Grand Teton National Park, while its northern and eastern borders extended far enough to include Jackson Lake and several smaller lakes, a 20-mile (32.2 km) stretch of the Snake River, and large sections of forest and sagebrush. Jackson Hole National Monument basically enjoyed the same protections and had the same restrictions as a national park—including bans on hunting and livestock grazing—but its creation did not require congressional approval, which had been the roadblock in the past.

This sent anti-park factions into an uproar. A bill to abolish the new monument quickly passed though both the House and Senate, but Roosevelt refused to sign it. Then, the state of Wyoming wanted the NPS to overturn Roosevelt's decision, but the NPS did not. Since they couldn't get the law on their side, some decided to disobey the law. Ranchers drove their cattle herds through monument lands. USFS workers stripped their ranger stations of equipment, supplies, and furniture before the buildings were turned over to the NPS.

Although people who lived closest to Grand Teton and Jackson Hole remained upset about the monument, the rest of the nation cooled off. In the late '40s, Wyoming legislators tried to eliminate the monument, but the U.S. government turned the other way. In 1950,

Horses (and cattle) from some of the area's private ranches are allowed to graze inside the park during the summer.

Congress agreed to merge Jackson Hole National Monument and Grand Teton National Park into the single 485-square-mile (1,256 sq km) park that exists today.

Today, bison herds may be seen making their way through Grand Teton's famous Mormon Row Historic District.

The detractors did not go away empty-handed, however. To this day, Teton County receives additional funds from the federal government, limited elk hunting is allowed within park boundaries, certain park areas are open to livestock movement and grazing, and a few existing residences and businesses have remained in the park. Also, there is a special law barring any president from ever again creating a national monument in the state of Wyoming.

Around the same time as the merger, other changes were taking place in the park. The year 1948 saw the creation of Jackson Hole Wildlife Park, an area consisting of fenced enclosures for elk and bison. The arrangement allowed wildlife biologists to study the animals and served as a tourist attraction at the same time. Some people contended that keeping animals penned in conflicted with the purpose of national parks. Although this was a source of controversy for two decades, the bigger story involved the bison.

No bison were living in Jackson Hole when the first settlers arrived, so when about a dozen bison broke loose of the wildlife park's fences in

Canada thistles and other nonnative plants tend to pop up and thrive after natural events, such as fires or floods, disturb the land.

1968, they were the first of their kind to roam free through the valley in at least a century. Park officials ultimately decided to allow the bison to wander anywhere in Grand Teton, and the animals' enclosures were done away with. In the decades since, the bison population has swelled to about 1,000. However, wildlife officials believe 500 is a healthier number to maintain, based on available food for the huge animals. Numbers in recent years have been reduced in part by hunting in the National Elk Refuge, where Grand Teton's bison congregate in the winter. These hunts are controversial, and protecting animals in one federally managed area only to let the same animals be hunted in another strikes some as self-defeating.

By and large, the addition of bison to Grand Teton has been a positive one. But the introductions of other new species aren't as welcome. Plants, such as Canada thistle, are often the most troublesome. They out-compete native species for water and sunlight and ultimately choke them out. While a casual human visitor may not worry too much about weeds and grasses in any given place, changes in ecosystems also affect the animals that eat the plants or seek shelter among them.

Nonnative plants are often introduced accidentally, and seeds may be carried hundreds of miles by human vehicles. But Grand Teton's issues with nonnative fish are not so accidental. To improve fishing in the area, various trout species were deliberately introduced into lakes. Anglers enjoy catching these fish, but the introduced species have taken over the space and food supply of the cutthroat trout, which is the area's only native trout species. Both plant and fish species are difficult to regulate once they've taken hold, and managing these nonnative species is an ongoing battle.

A species whose return provoked mixed reactions is the gray wolf. In 1995, the endangered wolves were reintroduced into Yellowstone National Park. As is their nature, the wolves began forming separate packs and establishing territories that sometimes covered more than 100 square miles (259 sq km) apiece. As the population grew, new packs spread farther outside Yellowstone's borders. By the late '90s, wolves had reached Grand Teton for the first time in about 70 years. Their arrival restored some natural balance to the park, as the predators kept down inflated elk, deer, and bison numbers.

However, just as the wolves wandered into Grand Teton, they could easily roam out onto private property or into the surrounding national forests or elk refuge—fences have little success in containing wolves. Nearby landowners have worried that their livestock or pets may be killed by the wolves. And neither hunters nor hunting-related businesses appreciated that the wolves were reducing surplus elk and deer populations.

By 2012, 6 separate packs—totaling more than 50 wolves—resided in the park. That same year, Wyoming deemed that populations throughout the state were high enough to justify a wolf-hunting season. Hunting wolves within Grand Teton is still outlawed, but many of the park's wolves have been legally shot near park's borders. These have included animals that wore radio-tracking collars and were being studied by wildlife biologists. Conservationists argue that there should be a no-hunting buffer zone around Grand Teton and Yellowstone, so that wolves living primarily inside the parks will be better protected when they venture outside their boundaries.

Gray wolves have fluffy outer fur that varies in color from white to black in addition to a thick layer of underfur for warmth.

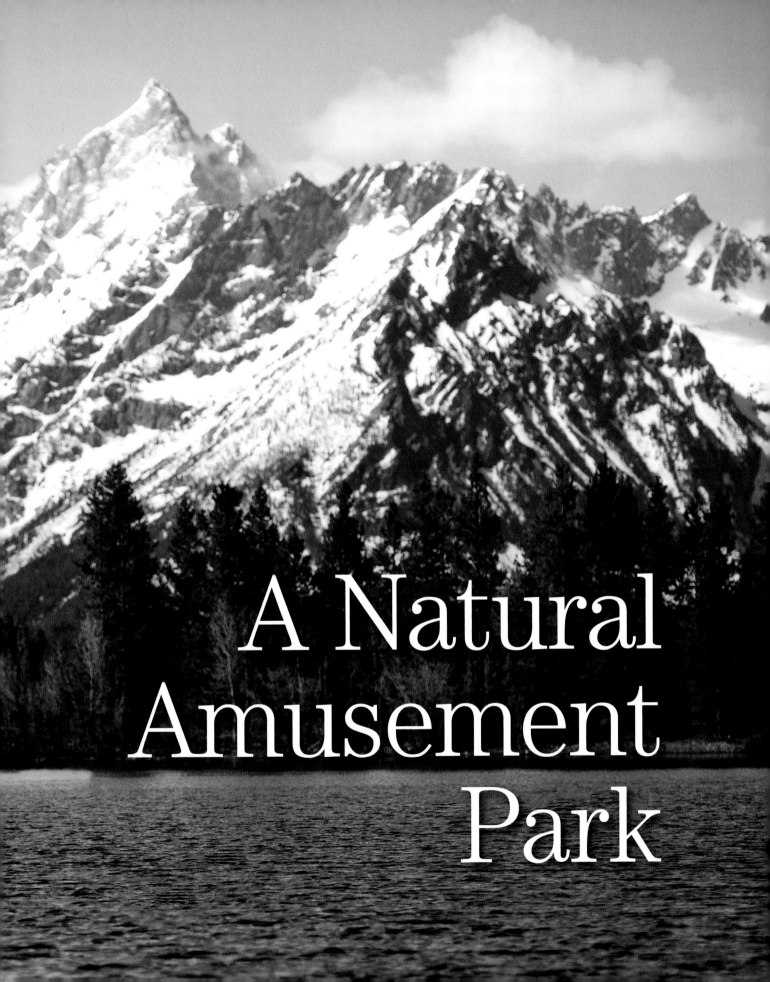

A Natural Amusement Park

In 2013, Grand Teton National Park drew in 2.7 million visitors. Some of its popularity is attributed to its proximity to Yellowstone National Park, which sees even more guests than Grand Teton. Some visitors to the region simply drive through Grand Teton as an afterthought following their stay in Yellowstone. Many others spend more than a day soaking up the scenery and pursuing the various activities available.

The majority of the guests come during the summer, when daily high temperatures average a pleasant 77 °F (25 °C). September and October boast smaller crowds while still achieving reasonably comfortable temperatures. Autumn months also feature bright yellow and orange leaves and the eerie bugling of bull elk seeking mates. From November through May, the weather tends to be wet or snowy, and even getting into the park in winter is not guaranteed. Regardless of when guests come, mornings tend to be the best time to be up and about. When the sky is clear, the rising sun illuminates the Teton Range, and the reflections cast a glow over the valley below. In the evening, the mountain peaks block out the western sun as daylight vanishes abruptly.

Those visitors who can manage only a quick tour are still treated to some of the most scenic drives in the world, and frequent pull-offs offer excellent vantage points for snapping photos. Two main roadways run northeast to southwest through Jackson Hole and connect to form a loop. The more westerly road passes by both Jenny Lake, which provides spectacular reflections of the Cathedral Group, and the Chapel of the Transfiguration, a picturesque church built in 1925. The eastern route runs along the winding Snake River and provides vistas of the river, scrub brush, and forests, all backdropped by towering mountains. Bison, elk, pronghorn, and occasional moose feed along this stretch. Additionally, several visitor centers, lodges, gas stations, restaurants,

Once Jackson Lake's ice thickens enough, visitors cross-country ski, hike, snowshoe, and ice fish on the frozen water.

Moose frequent the ponds and lakes of the Tetons, feeding on water plants as well as twigs, leaves, and other vegetation.

Grand Teton's trails and footbridges (below) afford hikers countless dramatic sights, including Hidden Falls (opposite).

gift shops, picnic areas, and restrooms are spaced along the main roads.

Since most of Grand Teton's paved roads are wide open with fairly gradual hills, they make safe, enjoyable routes for cyclists. Travel on unpaved roads is also allowed but may require mountain bikes. Cyclists are not permitted on hiking trails but are allowed on a 16-mile (25.7 km) multi-use trail that runs from Jenny Lake to the southern border of the park. Visitors can bring their own bikes or rent them within the park.

Visitors who opt to explore on foot may choose from about 40 hiking trails covering 250 miles (402 km). These trails range in length from 0.3 to 25 miles (0.5–40.2 km) and lead hikers along lakes, canyons, forests, wetlands, and waterfalls. Some of the most popular short treks begin near the Cascade Canyon **Trailhead**. This lies on the west side of Jenny Lake and can be reached by walking two miles (3.2 km) from Jenny Lake Visitor Center around the southern lakeshore or by riding a shuttle boat. Then an additional 0.6-mile (1 km) jaunt will lead to Hidden Falls. This 200-foot (61 m) waterfall cascades over a series of rocky drops and is framed by tall lodgepole pines. Just a little farther up the trail is Inspiration Point, which offers an unobstructed view over Jenny Lake and the valley beyond.

Those who continue along Cascade Canyon Trail and connecting trails can get closer views of the Cathedral Group, visit Lake Solitude nestled among mountain peaks, or see the Schoolhouse Glacier. Hikers to these and other remote locations often use the various **backcountry** campsites in the western and southwestern sections of Grand Teton. Day hikers who are more interested in wildlife tend to have better luck near the Jackson Lake Lodge area to the north. Numerous crisscrossing trails originate near here and wind along many lakes, ponds, and streams. While this area does not provide the best mountain views, the lusher

vegetation attracts more animals, including waterfowl, moose, elk, bears, and wolves.

Horseback riders also have access to most of the hiking trails, with some notable exceptions, such as the Hidden Falls and Inspiration Point paths. Horseback riders tend to prefer the longer trails toward the southwestern edge of the park, and those making multi-day trips can camp at one of five backcountry horse camps. Three riding stables within the park offer docile horseback rides to those people who don't own horses.

Grand Teton's many lakes and waterways provide additional forms of entertainment. Swimming is allowed but not widely practiced, because most of the water is rather cold, even in midsummer. But trout appreciate the cold water, and fishing is popular throughout the park. Visitors can buy the required Wyoming fishing license and some supplies at various stores within the park. Different lakes and streams have varied regulations about limits and bait use, so anglers should inquire at a visitor center before wetting a line.

Guests may bring their own boats into Grand Teton or rent various watercraft within the park. Motorized boats are allowed only on Jackson Lake and Jenny Lake. Non-motorized boats, rafts, canoes, and kayaks may be used on all the park's sizeable lakes and on the Snake River. Floating down the Snake River in rafts or kayaks is a popular activity, and different stretches of river are categorized as beginner, intermediate, or advanced, according to the speed and roughness of the current. Guests can take on the river independently, but guide services are also available.

Rock climbing is another draw of Grand Teton. The granite slopes of the mountains are ideal for climbing, and the park attracts serious climbers from around the world. Like floating, this activity can be beyond the skills of some park visitors, but outfitters within

Rangers remind anyone enjoying the park's wildlife (opposite), scenery, or physical activities (below) to be alert.

the park can provide equipment, lessons, and close supervision to ensure that novice climbers have a safe, enjoyable experience.

The relatively rare winter visitors to Grand Teton are treated to a unique view of the landscape and different experiences. This is a quiet time of year, and wildlife often stands out against the white backdrop of snow. Guests have about 50 miles (80.5 km) of groomed ski trails at their disposal, or they can blaze their own paths in most parts of the park. Those wanting more speed can take guided or unguided snowmobile rides throughout much of the park. Ice fishing and snowshoeing are other common activities.

Those hoping to snowmobile through Grand Teton should check at a visitor center for maps, routes, and current regulations.

With so much to do and see, many guests opt to spend several days in Grand Teton. To accommodate these visitors, the park has around 750 lodge rooms and cabins at 7 different locations. Options include Jackson Lodge, where simplified décor takes a backseat to the surrounding mountain scenery. Other areas feature rustic log and tent cabins, and visitors can even stay at a dude ranch. Wherever guests choose to lay their heads, reservations are strongly recommended.

Campers have more than 900 sites in 5 campgrounds available to them. Campgrounds near Colter Bay have the most amenities, including RV hookups and shower and laundry facilities. Jenny Lake is the smallest campground and offers only tent sites. Prime scenery and more privacy between sites keep this campground filled most of the summer. None of the campgrounds takes reservations, so registering early in the morning is necessary to get into Jenny Lake or to get preferred sites in other campgrounds. All campsites feature picnic tables, fire rings, and bear-proof boxes in which to store food.

To visit Grand Teton today and see its breathtaking scenery and majestic wildlife and to immerse oneself in the region by scaling mountainsides, wandering through forests, or bouncing over river rapids, it is difficult to comprehend that the park's creation faced stubborn opposition for more than 30 years. But perhaps this was an important lesson in persistence. Today, visitors can appreciate not only the purple mountain majesties and the vibrant valley below, but they can also better value the fruits of the hard work that has helped preserve America.

Grand Teton's largely untamed landscape provides campers and other visitors with an unforgettable experience.

WARNING
August 2011
BEAR
FREQUENTING AREA
Removal of this sign may result in INJURY to others and is punishable by law
THERE IS NO GUARANTEE OF YOUR SAFETY WHILE HIKING OR CAMPING IN BEAR COUNTRY

Homely Swamp Dwellers

With its wide-set eyes, bulbous nose, knobby legs, and beardlike dewlap, the largest member of the deer family is also perhaps the strangest. Moose are up to 7 feet (2.1 m) tall at the shoulder and weigh as much as 1,800 pounds (816 kg). Males—called bulls—develop broad, scoop-shaped antlers that can weigh 70 pounds (31.8 kg). Moose are typically solitary, and females (cows) raise one or two calves at a time. Moose can run up to 35 miles (56.3 km) per hour and are powerful swimmers. They rarely stray far from water, where they do most of their feeding.

Coordinated Killers

Gray wolves were once erased from most of the U.S. but are making a gradual comeback in a few northern regions, including Grand Teton. A grown wolf can weigh more than 125 pounds (56.7 kg) and sprint 35 miles (56.3 km) per hour. It also has keen senses and impressive stamina. Both powerful and persistent, wolves typically hunt in packs of around 6 to 12 individuals. They generally target very young, very old, wounded, or sick deer, elk, moose, or bison, but they will hunt healthy adults of those species if easier options aren't available. They nearly always avoid humans, however.

Leaving Humanity, Seeking Wildlife

Grand Teton visitors who want to get away from crowds, stretch their legs, and increase their chances of seeing elusive wildlife may want to hike around Two Ocean Lake. The trailhead of this 6.4-mile (10.3 km) loop can be reached by taking a short, unpaved road off Pacific Creek Road at the eastern edge of the park. The trail follows along the lakeshore and passes through lush meadows and forests. The combination of water source, food source, and shelter in this area appeals to elk, deer, moose, and bears. A picnic area at the trailhead can make Two Ocean Lake a multipurpose stop.

Effortless Sightseeing

Various **concessionaires** *within Grand Teton offer rafting equipment and services to visitors, and guided tours on the Snake River are an excellent way to view and learn about the park. Many trips start at the Snake River Overlook and end at the park's Moose Village. The winding*

river offers constantly changing viewpoints. For two or three hours, guests can enjoy the ride, take in the mountain scenery, and try to spot bald eagles, beavers, elk, bison, and moose near the river's edge, while guides navigate the water and share information about the park. Some tours even stop for meals along the way.

Wildlife's Winter Home

Winter visitors to Grand Teton National Park are few and far between. The same is true of the park's elk during the coldest months. Most of them migrate to lower, warmer grounds in the National Elk Refuge just south of Grand Teton. Six to seven thousand of these majestic animals voluntarily crowd into the 39-square-mile (101 sq km) refuge each winter. The refuge has limited roads for wildlife viewing, but horse-drawn sleigh rides through the vast elk herds are offered to visitors. Passengers also might have the opportunity see bison, wolves, bighorn sheep, and bald eagles that winter in the refuge.

Wonderful Waterworks

Grand Teton's close neighbor to the north is Yellowstone National Park. Yellowstone features much of the same wildlife, similar prairies and forests, and some lakes and rivers. But what Yellowstone is best known for is its

hydrothermal activity, in which water heated to high temperatures underground results in unusual sights, sounds, and even smells at the surface. Boiling pools, hissing steam vents, and bubbling mud holes can all impress visitors, but the most popular hydrothermal features are the geysers, which periodically erupt, spraying huge volumes of water as high as 300 feet (91.4 m) in the air.

Not-So-Gentle Giants

Grand Teton visitors are often wary of the park's bears and wolves, but they tend to be less concerned about its herbivores. Bison, moose, and elk can appear tame and oblivious to humans, but all are big, fast, and capable of aggression. The bulls of each species are especially excitable during their rut—or mating season. For bison, this is midsummer to early fall. The rut for moose and elk is in the fall. Female bison and moose are more dangerous in the spring, when they are fiercely protective of young calves. Guests are advised to stay at least 25 yards (22.9 m) away from these giants.

Knowing One's Limits

In a world increasingly preoccupied with warning labels and safety regulations, Grand Teton manages to remain risky. Falls from steep mountain slopes, serious wipeouts in river rapids, and cases of **hypothermia** *all occur in the park every year. Many of these incidents stem from overconfidence, as visitors see experienced* **mountaineers**, *boaters, and backcountry hikers make physically demanding activities look easy. Because no rules prevent novices from attempting the same feats, many Grand Teton visitors find themselves in sticky situations.*

Guide services are highly advised for climbing and rafting, and hikers unused to rugged trails and map reading should stick to shorter day hikes until they better understand their capabilities.

Glossary

backcountry: an area that is away from developed or populated areas

botanists: scientists who study plant life

concessionaires: people or organizations operating businesses on sites owned by someone else

dude ranches: ranches operated primarily as a vacation resort, typically catering to clients with minimal knowledge of ranch operations

ecosystems: communities of animals, plants, and other living things interacting together within an environment

erosion: wearing away by the action of natural forces such as water, wind, or ice

foothills: hills that stand between a higher mountain or range and the lowlands around it

glacial period: any period in history when ice covered much of the earth

hypothermia: lower than normal body heat due to prolonged or severe exposure to cold

igneous: describing rock that formed when magma within the earth cooled and solidified

metamorphic: describing rock that has changed because of extreme heat and pressure

mountaineers: people who climb mountains for sport

philanthropist: a person who donates money in an effort to improve society or human welfare

tectonic: relating to the shifting, colliding, and separating of enormous slabs of the earth's crust

topographers: people who study the physical features of the land and make maps

trailhead: the starting point of a walking or hiking trail

Selected Bibliography

Kevin, Brian. *Yellowstone and Grand Teton National Parks*. New York: Random House, 2009.

Laine, Don, Barbara Laine, Jack Olson, Eric Peterson, and Shane Christensen. *Frommer's National Parks of the American West*. Hoboken, N.J.: Wiley, 2010.

Mayhew, Bradley, and Carolyn McCarthy. *Yellowstone and Grand Teton National Parks*. Victoria, Australia: Lonely Planet, 2012.

National Geographic Guide to the National Parks of the United States. Washington, D.C.: National Geographic, 2009.

Schullery, Paul. *America's National Parks: The Spectacular Forces That Shaped Our Treasured Lands*. New York: DK, 2001.

White, Mel. *Complete National Parks of the United States*. Washington, D.C.: National Geographic, 2009.

Websites

Grand Teton National Park
http://www.nps.gov/grte/index.htm
The official National Park Service site for Grand Teton is the most complete online source for information on the park and includes tips for park sightseeing, activities, and safety. Park regulations, lodging information, and various maps are also provided.

National Geographic: Grand Teton National Park
http://travel.nationalgeographic.com/travel/national-parks/grand-teton-national-park
This site provides a concise visitor's guide to Grand Teton, complete with maps, photos, sightseeing suggestions, and links to other popular national parks.

Note: *Every effort has been made to ensure that the websites listed above are suitable for children, that they have educational value, and that they contain no inappropriate material. However, because of the nature of the Internet, it is impossible to guarantee that these sites will remain active indefinitely or that their contents will not be altered.*

Index